In *LOVE WHAT IS MORTAL* Norman Schwenk selects poems from more than 60 years of writing and publishing in the US and the UK.

'...ebullient, rapscallion, hilarious and tender, Norman Schwenk's poems sing with life...'

Maggie Butt on *Book of Songs*

'...it's the humanity that moves me, the various humanity—funny, sad, reflective, ribald...'

Jeremy Hooker on *Book of Songs* and *Cadillac Temple*

'...a stimulating read...they richly reward rereading...fresh, vibrant...'

Nigel Jenkins on *Cadillac Temple: haiku sequences*

'Norman Schwenk is a wordsmith of great quality, someone who can fix a moment or an idea and make it come alive on the page, taking the reader to places he never dreamed of going.'

Phil Carradice on *The More Deceived*

'... manages to make a poetry both live and true to a mythology that bears very much on contemporary issues.'

Stewart Brown on *The Black Goddess*

Norman Schwenk was born in 1935 in Lincoln, Nebraska and grew up there. Educated in the United States, he taught literature and writing at Cardiff University, Uppsala University in Sweden and the University of Pennsylvania in Philadelphia.

His most recent collections of verse are *The More Deceived: poems about love and lovers; Cadillac Temple: haiku sequences; and Book of Songs.* Married to the Welsh w   lives in Cardiff.

Love What Is Mortal

Selected poems

Norman Schwenk

Parthian, Cardigan SA43 1ED
www.parthianbooks.com
First published in 2016
© Norman Schwenk 2016
ISBN 9781910901786
Cover image by Jill Barker
Cover design by Richard Cox
Typeset by Elaine Sharples
Printed in EU by Pulsio SARL
Published with the financial support of the Welsh Books Council
British Library Cataloguing in Publication Data
A cataloguing record for this book is available from the British Library.

FOR DEBORAH

Foreword

The poems in this book are arranged roughly in chronological order. Each section is given the title of the original collection of poems: HATS, for instance, was my first collection, assembled in the 1960s; BOOK OF SONGS is my most recent, published last year. The final section, LOVE WHAT IS MORTAL, is not finished. I regard it as work in progress. Overall I have tried to make this a rigorous selection and hope there are not too many silver spoons gone out with the trash.

Norman Schwenk, 2016

CONTENTS

HATS

'Well?' demanded the King again.' Do you or do you *not* take off your hat before your King?'

'Yes, indeed, Sire,' answered Bartholomew. 'I *do* take off my hat before my King.'

'If that's your hat in your hand,' demanded the King, 'what's that on your head?'

Dr. Seuss The 500 Hats of Bartholomew Cubbins

HATS I

You speak to me now, please.
Tell me simply why she will not
Wear a hat.
A scarf sometimes, a cap perhaps,
But never, never a hat.
Tip-toeing Sunday ladies all but
Terrify her, and their daughters,
Who so happily put on their lady ways.
Then she asks me, 'Should I be a lady?'
At the Sunday zoo she and I
Saw how cute the tigress looked
With blue ribbon and a little
Plastic salad poised between
Her fabulous, pointed ears,
Propped above those awful eyes.

HATS II

Now none of the girls wear hats.
In imitation of her?
Though some have begun to wear them again
Since none of the others are.

For a new decade has arrived.
In fact it's already gone.
And girls will forever be taking off hats
And forever putting them on.

And my love forever stands apart.
I bought her a hat today
Because it was too cold outside
And she had an aching ear.

We went back to the zoo to watch
The tigers play in the snow.
Lord, I wish you could have seen them—
Tigers can really go.

They've got an island all their own
And when the snow is deep
They run and splash and wrestle and shout
Like children before sleep.

I won't forget her pleased surprise
On reading that snowy afternoon
How tigers are equally at home
In blizzard or monsoon.

So. Beat that. We won't try.
We sipped our blistering cups of coffee,
Bundled ourselves down to the station
And caught the train home, warm and cosy.

MORNING SONG

CHORUS: Good morning! *Corragio*!
                   Don't be mad or blue
                   Remember almost everybody
                   Feels as bad as you
                   But the sun goes right on shining
                   When it's stuck behind a cloud
                   And the birds go right on singing
                   Though they're awful fucking loud

I knew a man from New York
Who thought he was betrayed
Whose brother requisitioned
All the money he had made
And did a flit to Florida
And on down to Brazil
And left him with a lawyer
And a bag of unpaid bills

He went to see his mistress
To renovate his pride
To say though she was on her own
He'd love her till he died
But there pinned on her pillow
Was a note that made him ill
It said, 'Gone with an old friend
On a trip down to Brazil'

He went home to the wife and kids
To get away from guile
To tell the wife they'd start again
And take it with a smile
But she told him, 'You can start again
Go ride your hobbyhorse
I'm going down to Rio
And I want a quick divorce'

He went to see his doctor
Feeling like an oily cheese
He learned he had contracted
An incurable disease
But the doctor said, 'Don't worry
Every day take ten of these
Though it may hurt in the mornings
Live as long as you damn please'

DROWNING SONG

CHORUS: It takes a strong swimmer
          To save somebody drowning
          To bring them from the bottom of the sea
          Your loving arms are strong
          So say it won't be long
          Before you reach my hand to rescue me

I saw you on the beach today
You didn't even look my way
Your mind was on a million other things
I tried to wave and catch your eye
You didn't even hear me cry
'Hey, baby, have you got my water wings?'

I bought you peanuts and a coke
I thought we'd sit and have a smoke
And things might be the way they used to be
But you ran off and shut me out
You didn't even hear me shout
'Hey, baby, come on back, the treat's on me'

Who was that nerdy little rat
The one who gave your cheek a pat
And giggled when you chased him down the sand ?
How could you fool around that way
When I was floundering in the bay ?
Oh, baby, here I am, please take my hand

I'm going down a second time
You may be guilty of a crime
You act as though I'm bathing in a tub
But I'm a desperate drowning man
Oh take my desperate drowning hand
Oh, baby, blub blub blub blub blub blub blub

I dreamed I tried to make you fly. You were a flower,
and I thought you were a butterfly like me. I wagged
my wings as forcefully as a butterfly can, pulled and
lifted. 'She might be still stuck on a bit of cocoon,'
I said to myself. But you were held by many roots.
I couldn't see the roots. I only saw that you were
wonderfully like me and seemed to smile. I dreamed
of how we'd flutter the wide meadows together,
finding the best flowers and warning each other
away from killer sprays, just one perfect summer.
I thought of when I was only a little pupa, a dumb
chrysalis, when I learned the need for patience in a
loving task. So I held on and hauled. I tore my wings,
I tattered your petals. When I woke up we lay on
the ground together in many small shreds.

I am a still, expectant shore, waiting for you,
the sea, the next wave. It is hot here. I want
to scratch, my sand itches. I envy the drowned
sea bed, always immersed in you, always caressed.
When you draw back from me I run far out, as far
out as I must to hold you at my side, to keep your
touch, if only at the edges. The low tides are
rough and hard, almost intolerably dry. But you
return, always you return fresh, tenderly with a
soft rush, and I am smoothed and soothed, I am
cool again. I lie beneath you, bathed luxuriously
in your element. Now I am still. I must be very
still. I feel you moving, very gently moving
towards me.

TO YEATS, TOO LATE

Never give all the heart

Give all the heart. Give it all.
Don't shove it at her in a squall
Of blood and tears, though, and then expect
Her gratefully to snap up your delect-
Able organs, at your bloody beck and call.
No, no, you've got to watch and wait.
Give her a chance to see you might be great—
That if she doesn't want your love, OK.
This isn't a game; it's dead serious play.
So hide your pump behind your back and pray.
And try to stop shaking. Let her have a peek
If she seems curious about the leak
Drip-dripping-dripping—your red-penny drops.
But no overtures. Patience. Till she stops
On some baroque off-day and says, 'Hey, Jack,
I want that funny thing behind your back.'
Then give it up. Don't sliver off a slice
And ask her if she likes the smell, the taste.
Just give it all. Garnish it on a platter,
Take a deep, gurgly breath, and hand it over.

MEMO TO PHILIP LARKIN

...the wires
whose muscle-shredding violence gives no quarter.

Dear Mr Larkin, I read your poem *Wires*
Just recently, and was a bit non-plussed.
What you say is more than a bit unjust
About my home, which was the Wild West once.
It's true we do employ electric fence,
But there's no muscle-shredding violence.

Blunder against the wires—you feel a thump,
A gentle, strange, metallic *Tummm Bump*.
The cattle feel uneasy, shy away.
When I was a small boy we used to play
A game to see which kid would let go last.
I was a toaster making crunchy toast
From my mom's great homemade cinnamon bread.
Tummm Bump. Purifies the blood, they said.

THE BATTLE

But finally to the death I face my twin,
This bastard self, who seven years ago
Humiliated me, who with a cackle
And a last boot in the groin, left me for dead.

And I was afraid. For long months I hid
In a lone, dark room, going out in disguise.
Years I clung to a quiet path I hoped
Would avoid him. Simply, I'd had enough.

Then I met you, and knew he would come again.
When your arms kindled me I longed to meet him.
He strode swaggering in, strong, to take
His maiden shock of what you tendered me.

He is still strong, but now is the one who's scared.
He used to wade straight in—now he's sneaky.
Here I pause, chat with friends; his thumb
Begins to dig deep in my inner thigh.

Here he deftly almost gouges an eye.
Now on the street, his knuckle in my plexus.
And in bed at night, the time most fierce,
We snarl and bite and wallow jungle-style.

But for all his filthy tricks, I pity him—
More each night. I cracked his last molar
And felt the pain myself. His proud eyes
Are blackened out of sight. The rectum bleeds.

One arm hangs limp as a willow switch.
A sad mess, and yet I murder him—
No fair match, for you have touched me, you
Have made me stronger than my second self.

TO AN AMERICAN TOURIST

Drowned in Lake Lucerne in a tourist coach accident

At last you are not comic anymore—
Across my morning coffee, the front page.
Even this old colonel from the veldt,
Thick with scars,
Now being kicked upstairs and cheered on,
Stares dumbly at your column touching his.
It draws the pupils with a dull jar.
A soft signal rings on fluted plate,
Over my sunny breakfast room array,
Faintly, over surgical-white
Tablecloth, an air of stray
Marmalade, bits of scone,
Your strange last splashing comes.
Slow dust revolves in solid beams of light
And I,
I drop down quietly in Lake Lucerne.

I see your wristwatch first,
One hundred-fifty feet,
Eye of the moon; its tiny dial
Is still shining free of crust.
And you here seated for a ride,
So patiently, your hair long barley
Under the wind, flows gently away,
Then back. Around rise such usual
Things that made us laugh so:
Your slack-wire voice, the sturdy calves
On flats, the mild, muddled brow.
I see all the light will allow.

O tourist, tell me, whisper to me how,
How could your brief descent be endured?
The colonel here knows pain
And death in war—when he lay in ruts
With knee-caps cut clean by knives.
I have seen death squirm, tourist,
Squirm and wriggle on my front page.
I've grown yearly more inured
To evils dealt mere cities and the poor fish.
But look, the colonel and I, we gape at this
Like two star runners losing an easy race.
For you are a young woman, dead on a journey.
Deep water wept the labels from your face,
The luggage stickers and the unkind names.
You were suddenly a young woman,
Sleeeping, and beyond our niggard love now.

THE 'U' CERTIFICATE ALPHABET

When poets get regularly shouted down
it's good for their verse and health
but it's best for the safe and the precious to find
you're heckled by yourself

Adrian May The Braintree Test

A is for AARDVARK

Have you ever seen an aardvark?
They're like piglets, only hairy
They live in funny burrows
At the front of the dictionary

B is for BLIMP

I'd like to be a blimp
All squashy soft and floaty
I wouldn't be a rocket
All the money in your pocket
Wouldn't make me be a rocket
Always in a hurry
Shooting off somewhere
With shudderings and shocks
No, I'd like to be a blimp
And doze and go for lazy walks
Way up in the air

C is for CLUTTER

Do you love clutter? I do
It's always worth exploring
Old bits of clock and pieces of rock
Or a lock that may somehow unlock
But if you have to TIDY IT UP
It all appears DEAD BORING

D is for DEATH

Why are the grownups scared to talk?
When they dare, why do they lie?
It's Death, the Mystery Tremendous
Solved by you, tough Private Eye

E is for ELBOW

Neglected bit of skin and bone
The elbow is unloved, unknown
(Whose elbow have you ever kissed?)
Though a mere forearm and a wrist
Away from the most familiar land
The back yard of the back of your hand

G is for GHOST

We got a ghost in our house
A real live ghost that's dead
You feel her tickle on the hump of your neck
When you clump upstairs to bed
My folks, they don't believe me
They don't think ghosts are real
But you got to believe what you hear and see
And you got to believe what you feel
I kinda like our ghostie
I know she wouldn't harm a soul
But you feel pretty funny
Your tummy goes runny
When suddenly you're cold
And you smell a bit of mould
And your shadow on the wall
Looks very very very very old

I is for INDIANS

'They're Indians,'
Columbus clucks and smiles
And who in Spain will argue now?
Besides, he's only wrong
By fifteen thousand miles

K is for KNIGHT

A knight on horseback wielding a lance
Sealed in armour cannot dance
A dancer lithe in a leotard
Isn't even a match for the palace guard
Each has his place and each his uses
A fruit has rind and also juices

M is for MOTHER

Is mother an old mop?
Is father an old flop?
They're still your folks
Not dirty jokes
So whatever you're doing
STOP

N is for NIGHTMARE

Whether you're gripped
By a sticky glob
Or trapped in a flaming jet
No show can beat a good nightmare
No matter how corny or wet

O is for OGLE

It's impolite to ogle
Yet it's often done
Staring very rudely
Can be a lot of fun
Fun for me, fun for you
Grownups like it, children too
Blind as a newborn bat
You can still be ogled AT

Q is for QUICKSAND

It's great to see the Bad Guy slither
Slurping beneath the ooze
But why does the Good Guy
Scramble to save him
Sacrificing his shoes?

R is for RIDDLE

What small thing holds a gingko tree
With underneath a blue bass fiddle
With on the back right in the middle
A picture of you with a picture of me?
Answer: this riddle

S is for SEX

Another Tremendous Mystery
That makes the grownups mum
Another job for Private Eye
Have pity on the poor tough guy
Some mysteries are awfully dumb
The more of them you solve, the more
Mysterious they become

T is for TRAIN

Her speed is terrific but feels like a cradle
She rockets you tenderly, hums you a song
And sleep is so easy, waking so gentle
A waiter comes swaying and playing a gong

U is for UGLY DUCKLING

I knew an ugly duckling
Who discovered he wasn't a swan
He met a lovely lady goose
And felt his feathers go all loose
And the light began to dawn

V is for VALENTINE

I listened to your heart today
Ka-thumping wondrous fast
And prayed that it would go always
And no beat would be last

X is for X MARKS THE SPOT

Dig here, says the map—a pirate's bones
Lie guarding the treasure with silent groans
And so we dig, but the map's a fake
We drew ourselves when hardly awake
Never mind, it's fun. We found a splinter
Of sky-blue glass to brighten the winter
Some good brass buttons, part of a comb—
Real tortoise shell—and took it all home
The bones of a chicken raised absent hackles
Guarding the treasure with silent cackles

THE BLACK GODDESS

Nevertheless Ishtar, though the most powerful deity of her day, did not rule alone. At Hierapolis, Jerusalem and Rome, she acknowledged a mysterious sister, the Goddess of Wisdom, whose temple was small and unthronged...
call her the Black Goddess...

Robert Graves *Mammon and the Black Goddess*

MY FAULTS

I think about my many faults. It's hard.
Consider the great California fault. It's easy—
that ghoulish grave-in-the-making, which spells
eventual doom of cataclysmic proportions.
Imagining it is almost comfortable,
quite distant and abstract, like the dying sun.
But think of your own faults, think of turning
over a damp stone or a rotten log and saying
me, that's me, and you wouldn't want to touch it:
small, thousand-legged worms of vanity,
great slugs of sloth, grubs of self-indulgence;
see them writhe and scuttle to shun the light.
Fellow-creatures all, they want to live,
and who are we to shudder and stamp on them?

ROCAMADOUR

Here high up where the sun once looked upon her
this Black Madonna rules a humble realm.
The pilgrims who arrive are mostly tourists.
Decorum is lax—they leave their shoes on.
Her expressionless gaze sees right through them.
She doesn't smile. The infant on her knee
is not the object of her adoration.
Here is no mild, virginal white Mary,
nor savage goddess beckoning for blood.
Serene sister, daughter, bride and mother,
she looks beyond all that. Her church is small,
her supplicants few, her secrets well-chosen.
And if you dare breach her magic circle,
you enter through the fire that burns you black.

TREGYNON

A flying blast furnace disturbs the peace,
the RAF training over mid-Wales.
This is our summer holiday. It's raining.
Intelligent, serious people on TV
debate the trials and tortures of the Cold War.
An actress recites poems about Hiroshima.
It is calm and central here—Armageddon
hard to imagine, so huge to take in.
Apocalypse gets mixed up with trivia.
And really we're happy now together;
any death at all seems too cruel.
The cow next door is bawling for her calf:
he went to slaughter this morning—now I try
to comfort my daughter with clumsy words.

STILL LIFE

After we go to bed they hang around
as if half-hoping for another party:
a lone bubble rises and pops the surface
of Perrier water, flanked by lemonade
and 'afore ye go' whisky almost gone;
two wine glasses, raised on elegant stems
keep company with a plain crockery bowl—
comrades in emptiness; blue playing cards
poise to be played again, and cigarettes
anticipate being set on fire soon;
white frosted cake, studded with gold and silver…
something odd to munch in a plastic bag…
does anything at all depend on this?
It only goes to show there is still life.

ARIADNE IN PENARTH

When you opened the door you looked so different,
as though we'd loved each other in past lives.
Your eyes reflect the things we know together,
all of the rude, ghastly and lovely secrets.
'Tell me more,' you said. I took a long breath
and plunged into the frightful labyrinth,
holding tight to the single thread you gave me,
wondering if the monster still lived there.
'Am I shallow?' you ask. The cave is deep,
profoundly dark and tortuously winding.
Many small deaths later I reach the centre:
it is a vast beach lit by a full moon.
The monster lies curled like a cat, asleep,
and purring like a pool of loony frogs.

GREGYNOG HALL

I wonder whether ghosts of the dead sisters
still roam these corridors, exasperated,
wishing they had the whole thing back, and vaguely
searching the bedrooms for an honest man.
No spectral sightings have yet been reported,
no clankings, groans, mysterious moving objects,
no morbid smells nor columns of cold air;
and yet I feel strong presences in this house,
ghosts of my own: they disappear round corners;
their voices echo in the cobbled courtyard;
they look up smiling from a chair and vanish.
It's wrong to meet or mate with ghosts, I know.
It's cruel and sad to keep the dead alive,
but harder than ever now to let them die.

VAMPIRE

He is a kind of vampire of the heart.
He lives off the strong, iron blood of the young.
His fangs, long and yellowing with brown spots
adore to puncture the flesh of soft throats.
He sleeps through day; at night unfurls his wings,
grooms his nest and waits for distressed lovers.
They come seeking shelter; he gulps their blood.
Deep in hypnotic trance, they never miss it.
Do not say he gives nothing in return.
His thoughts flow into theirs and comfort them—
the wisdom of many long, harrowing lifetimes.
He gives them calm to weather the hard storms.
He suffers the hurt of laying bare his mind.
It is horrible to remember being young.

ROMCOM

I believe in the fifth reel, in the triumph
of true love—never mind the times our film
got stuck in the gate and horribly, slowly,
we watched it melt like a flower of Hell.
I believe in boy meets girl in the first
reel, and then boy loses girl in the second
or third, and then boy gets girl and they live
happily ever after, after the fifth.
Now she's upstairs asleep, fitfully snoring.
It's late in the fourth reel and God it's rough—
all the forgiving, the getting down to earth.
The first, second and third were Heaven and Hell,
but this is the tough part, the getting ready
to live in the real world after the movie.

GOLDEN CROSS

Those grey days when the daisies never open,
when gloom hangs heavy in the atmosphere,
when I go round grovelling in self-pity,
my bitter thoughts turn back to bitter beer.
Then I make for the pub, where I feel better.
It stills the loud, internal growls and yelps.
Confronted by obscene infernal daymares,
a thing that you can get a grip on helps.
Praise Bacchus, all that bullshit, if it works.
I do believe this dark-brown, glassy grail.
I know no earthly, deep, definitive answer
except to plunge deep in the dark of ale.
Here is no quest for Honour, Truth or Love.
This Beauty we can get to the bottom of.

SOAP OPERA

Washing our juices off me in the shower,
lathering in the love we made together,
I wonder if it's the last time, and whether
something survives, or it all goes down the drain.
Will our story be short, sad, abortive,
struggle to find a shape, then dribble away,
or can we in this life accomplish telling
tales that are beautiful and complete?
I step out of the shower, dry my body,
wrap a soft robe around me, brush my teeth
and walk into the garden, where it's morning.
Over the wall the sun should be coming up.
I gaze at the blue hills and scratch my head.
On the horizon is rising a huge question mark.

EPITHALAMION

He is the snake's-head lily and she the wild
brier rose. His love among men's is like
the blossom among cactus. His beloved
among women is like the flowering
cherry among winter spruce and pine.
He sat down at her feet and tasted and, Lord,
the fruit was sweet, sweeter than any fig
from Israel or melon from Alabama.
The crocuses and snowdrops came too early,
a false alarm, but the rare snake's-head lily
makes no mistake, he is spring, he will summon
the wild rose. Listen, can you hear the voice
of the turtledove? Spring wades the bluebells.
The sleepy coo of summer is on its way.

BEREAVEMENT

Footsteps outside my door; a car pulls up.
I listen hard. It's not you. Still, I listen.
Why this unavailing hope? It's masochistic.
What's the use of it beyond sheer self-torture?
'Bereavement is a normal form of madness.'
Am I insane, doctor? 'It has the symptoms:
anxiety, depression, gross disturbance
of function, obsessive-compulsive patterns
of behaviour.' What can be done to help me?
'I see this: a quiet street, an open window,
and white net curtains hovering in the breeze.'
What kind of answer is that? Is it Zen?
'Oh no, it means go look, listen and look
when you hear footsteps or a car pulls up.'

PEMBROKESHIRE CLIFF HIKE

All that day I followed her miles and miles,
dogged and faithful, like a veteran husky
follows the leader of his team, her bottom
bobbing along beautifully through the landscape.
What a bottom and, Lady, what a landscape—
the view surreal, a constant, changing dream,
magic lantern of her, sea, earth and sky
thrown in three dimensions and perfect colour.
Hard as I walked, I never once got closer.
Here was no mirage but a solid picture,
constantly receding as I advanced,
fading and growing fainter with the twilight.
And though she disappeared in the dark night,
I feel her spirit ahead, still tugging me.

BLACK MADONNA AT LLANDAFF

Mourned by the first eleven, true disciples,
who gather round her small bed looking stunned—
John holds a candle; Peter reads a psalm;
one hides his face deep in his hands, his grief
has burst out of him like a frightened grouse
out of a bush—at least she has their comfort,
consigned to suffer in this draughty aisle,
she has no niche nor altar of her own.
The crowd kneels to her Son, bold and ascending,
aluminium cast by the great Epstein.
She is oak, carved by a nameless craftsman—
oak stained black and blackened by centuries
asking the same question over and over:
how can the Mother of All Living die?

BLACKWEIR, RIVER TAFF

I give you this poem from the grave.
It is in darkness we can best see light,
if there is light to see. When children fear
the dark we comfort them and say, there, there,
nothing to be afraid of, it's all right,
I'm here, daddy's here, go to sleep.
And when you're humbled, scared like a child,
all alone in the night lane, with a black moon,
and clouds shrouding the stars, freaked by sounds
of hidden water, dreading the owl's who?
wishing to God you'd taken the main road,
when you're longing for light, for even a slight
resurrection, then you're ready to see
like a humble seed sees, and starts to move.

NO LIES

Your name is written on air, mine on water.
Soon we will mix with earth, or fly in fire.
Is it better to leave names cut in stone?
Isn't the lot of the dead to lie forgotten?
Breathe on a mirror—see how quick the mist
evaporates, leaving the same old face
glowering back at you like Fate itself.
How can a breath aspire to permanence?
The Dead, they do not need to be cajoled
with tales of how they soldier on in life.
They leave their mark, their ripple, their vibration,
and ask now to be left in peace … no lies
about immortality, nor death disturbed
with the undignified longings of the living.

DRUIDSTONE HAVEN

Quiet at last. Though I hear muffled voices,
giggling bedtime noise. The fridge starts up,
then shudders to a halt. Above the silence
whispers of feathered surf and flying moon.
Now is the time of night when things happen,
UFOs and witches, things unspeakable,
when people die in sleep and lovers wake
the one they truly love deep in the dark.
Good Goddess, bless our frail house; may we last
the night out to the day and far beyond.
We are good people, followers of yours
you might say, who are sworn by all that's holy,
by all we have done right and will do wrong
to mark this moment of stillness together.

HOW TO PRONOUNCE WELSH PLACE NAMES

I spende moare tyme onn thee M4
thann everre onn my wife before
David Greenslade *M Foure Mye Girlefrende*

A spinster of Abertillery
Lost Fifi, her favourite canary.
Fed up with her cage,
Fifi's earning a wage
Serenading the cows at the dairy.

A dauntless explorer from Bangor
Succumbed to a tropical languor.
No cause for rebuke—
It was simply a fluke
Picked up from a friend in Katanga.

Our builder from Betws-y-Coed
Really knows how to get us annoyed.
Since he poured the concrete
Of our garden love seat
We've been missing our chihuahua, Floyd.

There was an old tart from Caersws
Who was so prodigiously loose,
A man who fell in
Found a squatter named Flynn
And the crew of a lost plane from Rhoose.

A young New Age priestess from Clwyd
Got hooked on a hazardous fluid.
The upshot was weird—
She grew balls and a beard
And ended her days as a Druid.

A solicitor living in Clyro
Is proficient at forging a giro,
And with consummate skill
He can fiddle your will,
Then burgle your house with a biro.

A mason who hails from Crickhowell
Is missing his pinny and trowel.
They've gone down the throat
Of his best billy-goat
And established a lodge in the bowel.

A champion skydiver from Denbigh
Intended a touchdown at Tenby,
But high winds prevailed
And his parachute failed,
So now he shall never again be.

A sensitive kid in Llanelli
Is in love with Fiona Pitt-Kethly.
Her poetry reading
Has left his heart bleeding
And him in the pub looking deathly.

A shy vicar born in Llanfair
Was familiar with boys in the choir,
So under their robes
To parry his probes
We wrapped the lads round with barbed wire.

In wee Llanvihangel Crucorney
There lived a fair maid who was horny.
She just fancied a shove,
But the boys longed for love
And other stuff equally corny.

A pickled policeman from Laugharne
Has breath like the floor of a barn.
He can empty a bar
Asking how people are
And disperse angry crowds with a yarn.

A factory girl from Llanrwst
Told her foreman she loathed being goosed.
He was shocked she was peeved—
He sincerely believed
He was giving his workers a boost.

A seven-foot forward from Lleyn,
Gentle giant of Wales' first fifteen,
Met a pack of All Blacks
Who hit him like an axe.
Now he's fly-half for Hell, and he's mean.

A yuppy from near Nantymoel
Imported his own olive oil.
His fresh cannelloni
Were famed in Llanthony
As the best thing to bandage a boil.

There was a nice lady of Neath
Who was proud of her new set of teeth,
But ignored her advisers
And lost her incisors
While chewing baklava in Greeth.

An archbishop bound for Prestatyn
Discovered his hat had been shat in,
But an instant too late—
It was clapped on his pate
Before you could say 'wait' in church Latin.

A schoolboy who swam at Rhosili
Saw something appear on his willy.
Right in front of his eyes
It grew ten times its size
And then disappeared, willy-nilly.

A fisherman trawling Trawsfynydd
Cried out, 'Lord, my cup overrunneth!'
'My mirror-bright sturgeons
'Make lamps for the virgins
'And lo, the dark bridegroom, he cometh!'

A mistress from Ynysybwl
Thought her lover a bit of a fool.
After bonking, his nose
Would run like a hose,
Then he'd fall asleep snoring, and drool.

THE MORE DECEIVED:
poems about love and lovers

Hamlet: I loved you not.
Ophelia: I was the more deceived.

LOVE LIES WITH TRUTH

Love tried to live with Truth.
God, she found it hard:
He ranted in his sleep,
Left rubbish in the yard.

She tried to live without him.
That was even worse:
Waking beside utter strangers,
Telling lies in verse.

Now they share a house.
They've got it about right:
He sees her nearly every day;
She visits him at night.

All their friends agree.
Solicitors concur:
She's aimless without him;
He's heartless without her.

A SERIOUS LOVER

A serious lover felt a fancy
Undermine his soul,
Like a vast, velvet lawn succumbs
To a tiny, velvet mole.

He said, 'I'll fetch my mole-trap
With its wicked spring and dart,
Expunge this roguish fancy,
So unworthy, from my heart'.

So he scoured shed and attic …
It was nowhere to be found.
At last he realized his trap
Must still be underground.

Metal-detector man strode forth;
His robot-waddle gait
Surveyed each centimetre
With magnetic-magic plate,

But still no bloody mole-trap.
Where had the bastard gone?
He stopped to look. His raging eye
Beheld the ravaged lawn,

Dug up for coins and bottle-caps,
Five paperclips, one nail—
A hundred little black hills
And not one the mole-trap grail.

The mole soon strangely vanished.
And hanging from a hook
He found the trap in his garage
Where he'd forgot to look.

TWINS

Pain is the twin of pleasure—
One a sunny smile,
The other dark and secret, not
Welcome at the ball.

But they are true sisters.
Never come between.
They'll gobble you up, spit you out
And pick your bones clean.

Waltz with them till midnight,
Love them both to bits,
And have a brave face ready when
The glass slipper fits.

THANKSGIVING

'So now that I'm so fat,'
You ask me with a kiss,
'Can you still love all that?'

I gaze at so much bliss,
This you I do so love.
Is there some point I've missed?

Love, when push comes to shove,
The more of you there is,
The more there is to love.

RELUCTANT DRAGON

Those travel agents flash their wares
In lurid signs of puce and mauve:
Barbados, Goa, Graz, Tangiers—
Choose where the fickle heart shall rove.

My heart can only choose to cling.
It will not wander foreign parts.
Such strange names have a lonely ring—
My heart must beat beside your heart.

'Well, yes,' you say, 'but darling, dear,
The cord that links our hearts is strong.
Please, don't be dull, don't summer here.
Our heart-string stretches hard and long.'

So now I write to you from Rome.
It's hot here. Lots of ruins too.
I ponder the Fall and coming home,
The properties of guts and yew.

See, my heart stretches, far enough
To find it will not break when bent,
That two hearts can be supple, tough
And true as the famed longbows of Gwent.

BOSOM BUDDY

The goat of guilt sits on my chest.
He grins and dribbles down his chin,
So that his drops of spittle form
A rank pool that reflects his grin.

He fixes me with devil eyes,
Then sighs, exhaling brimstone breath.
I am the Great White Weight, he whispers,
Your bosom buddy, unto death.

FROM LLANDAFF WALK

3. Graveyard

Past the murder cottage
Where the Verger did his wife
(Electric fire in the bath
and down the drain for life)

The lovers walk the graveyard path—
No fear they will disturb
The slumber of the residents
Whose silence is superb.

A solitary raven perches
On an angel's locks.
He screeches 'Nevermore!' and points
To graves filled by the pox.

He might as well demand those cherubs
Stop their kissing game.
Their marble ears hear 'Evermore!'
All lovers are the same.

His name is Joy, the cherub boy—
The little girl is Hope.
Perhaps the Verger shall rise up
And wash their mouths with soap.

FROM LLANDAFF WALK

4. Tea Shop

This site may well be where a sacred well
Gave balm and zest to pagan penitents.
Here Christians built this cool Prebendal House,
And lively ladies of the W.I.
Serve tea and really splendid cakes and scones.

The lovers joke and natter with the ladies,
Then settle on the terrace to enjoy
Their tea and cake spiced with a silly question:
What can the 'P.H.' on the teacups mean?
Maybe the phrase that rhymes with 'cubic square'?

Right on cue the place fills up with school kids—
Huge and spotty, packed with rampant hormones.
The lovers flee; the ladies serving tea
Stop having fun to be grown up and boring.

FROM LLANDAFF WALK

5. Cathedral

Disguised as tourists, the lovers
enter a place where they have no place.
A chill air of unwelcome seems
to envelop them as the door shuts;
they hold hands for a little warmth,
feeling disdain in the eye of
Celibate Ascending gazing upwards
in the ascetic curl of his nostril.

Here is a place for warriors though,
a spare wayside chapel listing
exotic spots where soldiers killed
and died; the lovers know that sense
of being where you don't belong—
but how would it feel to die there?
A brace of clerics rattle off
some service, bang their books shut and scarper.

A place for the housewife surely,
this Martyr's chapel, shrine for all
down-on-the-knees doormat people.
Why else the votive Hoover left
standing on the scruffy, half-swept
carpet? The mild Martyr watches
pityingly from her window.
(At least, lovers, she knows where she belongs.)

Last, the Lady Chapel— perfect
for weddings—so pretty and
cheerful with its white art deco
virgin and child, its glittering
reredos in wood and gold leaf.
What a shame it makes the lovers
feel left out. I'm sure Our Lady
wouldn't want anyone to be excluded.

Still, maybe there is more in the air
than gouts of mouldy incense—
maybe change—and maybe even
change may have a human face:
Rossetti's triptych has been cleaned;
the mother's face, still careworn and
troubled, seems more clearly the face
of a real woman, not some painted saint.

The Black Madonna has been given
her own niche; she dies facing her
Son, comforted by the mourning
first eleven, warmed by bright
terraces of candles which seem
always to light themselves, as if
by magic, making you wonder.
The lovers light two candles, one for Joy
and one for Hope, and pray they will live on.

IF ROSSETTI READ DICKINSON

Must parting be a part of Love—
Inevitable end?
With gaudy leaves and autumn sheaves
Descending the U-bend?

Does Love's enemy lie out there,
Hunkering in the dusk,
Selling succulent goblin fruit
That smells of mould and musk?

We gaze beyond the Sea of Death,
Conning for paradise,
Dreaming we'll be together there—
Palm trees and Pimm's on ice.

These metaphors we all live by
They seem a touch naïve.
Why wipe your tears and blow your nose,
Then blame it on your sleeve?

Our enemy, Christina dear,
Must surely lie in us?
'Ourself behind ourself,' she said—
Emily had it sussed.

THE MORE DECEIVED

The less deceived are those
Who know that life is short,
That wilt awaits the rose,
That missions all abort,

That death's the only truth,
And love ends in the sod.
So much for blinkered youth
Who think they're close to God.

But we are more deceived,
And many miles from youth,
So let us love, my love.
It's better than the truth.

CADILLAC TEMPLE:
haiku sequences

is the wind Spirit?
it is like: invisible
pulling down great trees

are clouds Illusion?
they are like: hiding the road
cars appear like wraiths

is the moon Knowing?
it is like: through wind and clouds
hinting a bright face

after Kikusha-Ni

AUTUMN

our gingko tree knows
the coming of autumn by
the stink of her seeds

lollipop cops bloom
bright yellow again beside
the zebra crossings

swirling whirling shapes
like schools of fish herds of sheep
starlings flock to roost

travel agent girl
puts holidays further south
up in her window

a sycamore leaf
clips the bridge of my nose on
its way to leaf-mould

BED

mysterious ship
incomprehensible home
of the prone body

worried by your wheeze
your night-breathing whistle I
realize it's mine

I move my body
against your body calming
the sad mind-rattle

dawn chorus of gulls
ak ak ak eeeee ak ak
we cuddle closer

making our bed my
hand pauses on a warm spot
beside your pillow

BIRDS

at the cathedral
inside a bronze crown of thorns
five swallows nesting

seagulls dance on grass
mimic the beat of raindrops
and up pops breakfast

a black kite swings high
some invisible trapeze
people oooh and aaah

walking the canal
a heron stands and peers round
keeping just ahead

that magpie again
he's selling The Big Issue
at your kitchen door

BODY

body-embossing
in pink faux-celtic patterns
when she turns in bed

bang! she drops the soap
through the shower curtain slips
a dimply bottom

the way she hunches
her back to reach the mirror
doing her makeup

she studies her face
in the brass doorplate across
the quiet arcade

snap of snooker balls
she leans over the table
her breasts in the way

DISGUSTING

it falls in the loo
will you reach in to fetch it
or stand there gawping?

watching her eat chips
politically incorrect
feelings take over

changing their nappies
why is it less repellent
when they're your own kids?

the President on
TV calmly hunting a
bogey with his thumb

they fart in bed now
is it the end of romance
or the beginning?

FENNEL

a sniff of fennel
and he's a small boy munching
liquorice cigars

and then a big boy
chewing on plug tobacco
laced with aniseed

and so a young man
watching ouzo go cloudy
everything gets blurred

then in middle age
strung out—hitting the absinthe
hallucinogen

now in sage old age
a flavour in his garden
the scent of fennel

FLAT

discouraging smells
emanate from God knows where
musty yet dusty

our landlord is in
denial about those dark
frisbee-size damp spots

wood laminate floors
that curdle up and crackle
new they looked so fine

cold tap that slams shut
never mind the hot tap will
run lashings of cold

and when the household
slurry bubbles the wrong way
poopy patio

MOVIE

why have I spent so
much of my time witnessing
actors pretend things?

we are not actors
don't want to go down in flames
with people watching

the twin towers shown
as an establishing shot
saddens many films

the Empire State used
as an action location
gladdens many too

so why do I cry
when Kong faces the sunrise
softly thumps his chest?

NIPPLE

'clitoris is the
only human organ made
solely for pleasure'

says The Vagina
Monologues—so what about
his pointless nipples?

'useless as tits on
a boar' declares the farmer
but sows caress them

with their bristly backs
waking the spiral penis
to full arousal

in the shower his
nipples are erect and still
tender from last night

QUINTET

Quintet by Brahms who
played in brothels whose beard smelled
of smoking stogies

we remark how much
the pianist resembles
a bank manager

the violins wear
shiny suits like footballers
huge collars and ties

the viola has
pitted skin the cello long
bare sinewy arms

these be our gods who
make the music of Heaven
we patter our palms

RAIN

rain on the lean-to
roof makes light skittering sounds
tip-toeing rats' feet

lost in thought he stands
under the bus shelter just
where rain is dripping

a little afraid
waterfall roars on skylights
everyone looks up

silent rivulets
on the glass—we play a game
of raindrop races

after the dry spell
rain silvering our roof slates
reflects a full moon

REPETITIONS

if you love someone
you love their repetitions
who said that? Twain? Proust?

mornings when she says
there's something wrong with me I
can't seem to wake up

and when she's making
herself more lovely—what's more
important than that?

now I watch her brain
tick-ticking trying to keep
everyone happy

and when she says I
can't seem to get to sleep just
before zuzzing off

UNIFORM

going off to work
her puritan uniform
defeats its object

breasts straining in blue
gabardine—sensational
legs in sheer black tights

black leather court shoes
pushing up calves and buttocks
while slimming the foot

the total effect
is smart severe and trashy
discipline mistress

you said it, Randy
we can't conceal the leopard
in dull null navy

WAITING

waiting is like jail
somebody keeps you locked up
you squirm in your shell

he waits in the bar
she waits in the restaurant
they miss each other

amazing stone egg
laid by a real Welsh dragon
you've had a long wait

M & S queueing
she waits and pays attention
to being alive

waiting is useful
and loafing too—the best things
hatch from sitting still

WINDOW

a three-legged cat
galloping past our window
at least I think so

yellow street lighting
makes their faces hideous
just for a moment

woman with MS
unsteady but she's going
shopping looking chic

window box meadow
long blond grasses toss their hair
behind wooden blinds

the radio sings
through the air a lone snowflake
silently descends

BOOK OF SONGS

It's such a sad old feeling
The hills are soft and green
It's memories that I'm stealing
But you're innocent when you dream
Tom Waits Innocent When You Dream

AUTUMN LULLABY

Slumber, little stranger,
Child of family blood
Your mum and dad made you
Out of their own mud

Now you live among us
Sleeping in our care
You breathe the air
Drink the water
Eat the food we share

You give us back your laughter
Your listening, your noise
You lift us with your energy
The glistening of your eyes

Sleep can be so easy
Pray the bugs won't bite
Then let the night
Fill your body
Till you see the light

Slumber, little stranger,
Child of family blood
Your mum and dad made you
Out of their own mud

A WOMAN FOR ALL SEASONS (FOXTROT)

CHORUS: A woman for all seasons
              That's what I want to see
              I'll search until I find her
              And hope she fancies me

Crazy days of springtime
Summer with winter too
Once I had a girl like spring
So hot and cold she blew
You might suffer sunstroke
In the warmth of her embrace
And you could catch pneumonia
Simply standing in her space

Let-down months of summer
Promising all things nice
Once I had a girl like summer
Visions of paradise
Followed by disappointment
When her weather cast its spell
You never saw so much rain
Then it was hot as Hell

MIDDLE EIGHT: I love every season
                     Mother Nature sends
                     It's what her daughters do with them
                     Drives me round the bend
                     Summer autumn winter spring
                     The planet's in a whirl
                     While I look for a lady
                     Who's an all-weather girl

Autumn is about dying
However lush the trees
Once I had a girl like autumn
Had me on my knees
Had me on my back as well
And standing on my head
So mixed up it's lucky
She didn't have me dead

Sombre days of winter
Unless you like the dark
Once I had a girl like winter
Nothing made her spark
Her Christmas lights were faulty
Her guiding star was blurred
She could wipe a sunny smile
With just a mouldy word

CHORUS: A woman for all seasons
That's what I want to see
I'll search until I find her
And hope she fancies me

BOBO HOME

We have a cosy bobo home
Our rooms are full of junk
Our loft is rubbish to the roof
Won't take another trunk

We rent a storage cubicle
Where so much trash is piled
That when we try to get inside
It springs like something wild

We're sick of books that we won't read
Pictures that we won't see
Records we won't listen to
Old cups that leak your tea

We'll never wear these dated clothes
The shoes won't pinch our feet
This lamp will never light out way
The rugs we'll never beat

We'll never watch these dvds
They'll never get to Oz
This chair will have no bottoms on
No flowers grace that vase

At least we'll feel at home again
When Time has passed us by
We'll join that junkyard in the earth
Fly to that scrapyard in the sky

HOMELESS

A house is not a home without a loo
The workmen said they'd be a day or two
Now I haven't got a home
I'm a king without a throne
And my castle moat is full of one and two

A home is not a sofa and TV
The workmen said there'd be an extra fee
But you need a bath to be in
And you need a pot to pee in
What feels more fundamental than a wee?

A home is not a kitchen or a bed
They'd be another week the workmen said
But you won't smell like a flower
If you haven't had a shower
Your odour may resemble something dead

A house is not a home without a loo
The workmen say they don't know what to do
So I haven't got a home
I'm a king without a throne
And my moat's afloat with doody doody doo

KNOTS AND TIES

When I was a little boy
I learned to tie my shoe
Make a pretty tidy bow
Pull it tight and off I'd go
Skipping up and down the stair
Safe as houses, unaware
I might be tripping on a lace
And falling on my stupid face

When I was a bigger boy
I learned to tie my tie
Windsor, four-in-hand or bow
Every knot there was to know
Neckties weren't for rain and storm
Didn't keep you dry or warm
I'd step out sleek and proud and vain
To show the world my gravy stain

When I was a youngish man
I tied the tie that binds
Worked so hard to knot it tight
Souls and bodies to unite
Sheepshank, granny, hangman's noose
Slip and square—they all came loose
Nobody suffered more than me
From D-I-V-O-R-C-E

When I was an older man
I tied myself in knots
Want, disease, injustice, war
Every cause worth fighting for
I fought to put the world to rights
But I'd get knotted every night
And while I struggled every day
The old world went its merry way

And now I am an old man
I've done with knots and ties
I'm free of all that binding stuff
Don't tie me down—I've had enough
It's Velcro slip-ons for my feet
My turkey neck is bare as meat
One ready-knotted tie does fine
The black tie ready-stained with wine

LONESOME COWBOY

It's lonesome our here on the range
With only the cattle to sing to
No comfort by day, no wonder by night
And only my saddle to cling to

By day I see plains of brown grass
Whether rolling or flat, it looks endless
And droves of brown dogies are no company
They only remind you you're friendless

By night I can gaze at the stars
We all know the stars never bore us
I warble my song and the steers moo along
And the coyotes bark a fine chorus

Some cowboys coddle their horses
They think it's the kind way to treat 'em
But I made up my mind it's worse than unkind
When you know you might have to eat 'em

I see lovely ladies in town
They look away quick when I pass 'em
I may not be tough but I'm dirty and rough
And look like I'm apt to harass 'em

It's lonesome out here on the range
With only the cattle to sing to
No wonder by day, no comfort by night
And only my saddle to cling to

'L'

I love being 'L'
It's the one way to be
Such a wonder to hear
So amazing to see

Just look at an apple
Or listen to surf
How better prepare
To go under the turf?

The smile of your baby
Chestnuts in the park
The frown of your enemy
Bite of a shark

Feel sun after rain
And rain after drought
A frosty full moon
Fresh air in your mouth

So lovely to lie in
And cuddle your mate
And have a good session
And laugh at your fate

Lovely to get up
And fly like a kite
Work you believe in
Fight the good fight

The lance of a surgeon
The glance of a friend
Good food good drink
Days without end

It's great to be 'L'
Be brave be bold
And make up your mind
To live, and die old

NO ROOM AT THE INN (CAROL)

No room at the inn
Tonight we have frost
Our babe nearly born
My wife needing rest

Sleeping in a barn
With her by my side
It's snug and it's warm
Pray God will provide

I feel the babe turn;
Rustling the straw
My wife gives a moan
And I am in awe

The three of us here
The Caesar's tax paid
And wonder of wonders
The child we have made

REFRAIN: Now sleeps the red rooster, now the white hen
The grey donkey shuffles and snores in his pen
They rest from labour, my wife's now begins
Our babe is ready, no room at the inn

NOT DELETED YET

Waiting for the doctor
She'll listen to my lungs
Say they're sounding better, not
Filling up with gunge

She'll say my heart is doing stuff
It shouldn't do at best
I'll smell of old Chanel—her button
Chilly on my chest

She'll twiddle her computer
While I fiddle with my clothes
Say I'm not deleted yet
From files God only knows

'O'

I hate being 'O'
Such a crap way to be
You can't see or hear
Takes forever to pee

Neck like a chicken
Teeth coloured grunge
Knees like noodles
Schlong like a sponge

Your zipper's half-mast
Your face is a wreck
Invisible now
To the opposite sex

And if you're a woman
Even a wag
You give in to gravity
All the bits sag

Your wrinkles grow wild
Like weeds on a tip
And for whom the bell tolls
Rings out when you strip

Crap waiting your turn
Uncertainty's certain
Whang! goes a loved one
Gone for a burton

Crap being trapped
On the very top rung
So make up your mind
To jump, and die young

PHILTRUM

Why have poets neglected thee
And lovers seem so bored?
Is it the mystery of your mark
That means you are ignored?

In the gauzy morning light
The rim of her philtrum glows
Satin lips her overbite
Beneath the legendary nose
And brow so white

Say, what is a philtrum for?
Is it a mere sluice for snot?
Not when it's one you adore
Cover with kisses moist and hot
It must be more

Are they baffled, pass you by
To praise a pink rosebud lip
A swelling breast, sparkling eye
Not your lovely, curious dip
I wonder why

Why have poets neglected thee
And lovers seem so bored?
Is it the mystery of your mark
That means you are ignored?

SHORT WAY HOME

We take the short way
Always the short way
We can't wait to get home
We take the short way
Always the short way
We always take the short way home

Soon we'll be off to Paris
Seems the right thing to do
After a long cold dark winter
Not everyone got through

We'll climb the little mountain
Visit the Sacred Heart
Lunch at our favourite café, the one
Built by the royal tart

We'll sit and sip our cocktails
After we stroll for miles
Floating past are unknown faces
Telling their unknown tales

It's great to go to Paris
Londontown or Rome
Berlin or Barcelona
But we take the short way home

We'll shop on the little island
Maybe find something chic
Browse the giant bookstore, the one
We'd like to browse all week

We'll see some famous pictures
Gaze at the golden dome
Say goodbye to cons and tricksters
Then take the short way home

      We take the short way
      Always the short way
      We can't wait to get home
      We take the short way
      Always the short way
      We always take the short way home

TIGER BAY: THE ALTERNATIVE TOUR (REGGAE)

O our Tiger Bay
We love Tiger Bay
Let 'em change her name
She won't be ashamed
Of her youth so fast
Of her dubious past
She will always be our Tiger Bay
We will always love our Tiger Bay

Here's a bronze of Ivor Novello
And his songs, romantic and mellow
Not dead on the page
He sings on the stage
Of the musical armadillo

Here's a church made of Norwegian wood
With a Welsh roof to shelter the good
Captain Scott nearby
Continues to die
With his men like a real captain should

Here's a bank that's still serving money
Not pina coladas with honey
Go on, order cash
They'll top up your stash
Or say no, are you being funny?

Here's a Nissen hut, stylish but bleak
What a shame there's no name—it's unique
It won a big prize
For architect guys
Who design sewage pumping with chic

Here's a fountain they call The Flourish
Both body and soul it can nourish
Have tea and a tart
And shop for some art
Feel free, have a pee, flush and flourish

O our Tiger Bay
We love Tiger Bay
Let 'em change her name
She won't be ashamed
Of her youth so fast
Of her dubious past
She will always be our Tiger Bay
We will always love our Tiger Bay

WEDDING BELL BLUES (KLEZMER SONG)

CHORUS: Wedding bell blues
Wedding bell blues
When you got it all
You got it all to lose
Don't stop and worry
Keep moving your shoes
Dance away the wedding bell blues

Solomon and Sheba had wedding bell blues
They had a lot to give and had a lot to lose
They might have lost it all if they hadn't been true
But Solomon was wise and Sheba was too
And when they said 'I love you' there wasn't no schmooze
They danced away the wedding bell blues

Anthony and Cleo had wedding bell blues
They had a lot to give and had a lot to lose
They might have had each other and the Valley of the Nile
But wanted all the world and wanted it in style
They gambled all for love; the Romans turned the screws
And they lost it to the wedding bell blues

Darcy and Elizabeth had wedding bell blues
They had a lot to give and had a lot to lose
Lizzie had her pride but she loved him tenderly
Darcy loved her back but was Lord of Pemberley
Finally they kissed and started moving their shoes
And danced away the wedding bell blues

Mickey Mouse and Minnie have wedding bell blues
They have a lot to give and have a lot to lose
Fiancés forever they've been courting so long
And never got married and you wonder what's wrong
They need a klezmer band and lots and lots of booze
To dance away the wedding bell blues

Little Ken and Barbie have wedding bell blues
They have a lot to give and have a lot to lose
Only made of plastic they have to use their wits
They've loads of accessories but no naughty bits
Their story's up to you; it's up to you to choose
What they do with the wedding bell blues

WHITE PLASTIC CHAIR

CHORUS: O the white plastic chair
It will always be there
When they dig us up, monument and steeple
Millennia from now
Prepare to take a bow
We'll be renowned as The Plastic Chair People

When politicians meet
They stand up on their feet
And talk about a world that's right and fair
But before the talking's done
The fighting has begun
To get their bottoms on the white plastic chair

When high-ups of the churches
Come down off their perches
Announce it's time for rich and poor to share
Where have they got their buns?
Why go to Sally Lunn's?
You can have them in a white plastic chair

When a judge holding court
Criminal or tort
Is sorting out the miseries of Job
You'll find him high in air
In a white plastic chair
That's slyly hidden underneath his robe

When a Lord of Fourth Estate
Finds another Watergate
He'll buy it if he's got a soul to sell
But why is it for sale?
It isn't Chippendale
It's plastic, white, and comes in green as well

When professors will process
In medieval-modern dress
And dole out their degrees to those who pass
It's the white Professor's Chair
That's waiting way up there
The throne to fit the academic ass

In a desert far away
From the heartless human fray
Where I had space to think and time to spare
I met an ancient Gypsy
Selling rum and Pepsi
And got tipsy in his white plastic chair

LOVE WHAT IS MORTAL:
elegy quintets

To live in this world

you must be able
to do three things:
to love what is mortal;
to hold it

against your bones knowing
your own life depends on it;
and, when the time comes to let it go,
to let it go.

Mary Oliver *In Blackwater Woods*

ANNE

funny how you seemed
to fit in with this bunch of
literary guys

without becoming
a substitute man—never
less of a woman

we were a little
in awe of you I believe
you stuck to your guns

yet had an easy
touch— no energy wasted
on ego trips or

hasty conclusions
there was always time for your
rich rolling chuckle

COLIN

'Cheers' you say and go
ahead of us the way you
did on weekend walks

we meet at the church
dedicated not to God
but to a writer

forget little urns
your ash comes in a big box
slippery gritty

boosting our bluebells
in the Wood of the Gentry
but I miss your laugh

we read your poems
in a clean well-lighted place
your book sells like beer

FRANK

you were a puzzle
in denial of your name
was it a surprise

when your cause of death
was a complete mystery?
'He just died,' she said

behind the hustle
of football, novel-writing
teaching, cookery

where were you, my friend?
so genial and generous
struggling to write

like the rest of us
but cursed with not being there
before you were gone

IRIS

you took on the snobs
ones like me who corrected
your punctuation

though you'd made maybe
millions selling your novels
in supermarkets

you had a good brain
and swept away the clichés
when it suited you

or conjured an age
when lonely hearts took weapons
and went out hunting

you silenced the snobs—
honorary doctorate
and a real M.A.

KARL

I saw you smile once
your graduation photo
at the crem chapel

a First in Sculpture
you mounted everyone's show
but never your own

'take care of yourself'
I'd say when we bid farewell
but you just wouldn't

you looked after us
instead—us and your family
DIY angel

who worried about
the rising damp in our walls
and not in your lungs

KATE

you came to my door
in the middle of the night
looking for your man

I'm sorry I lied
said he'd be home tomorrow
when I knew better

I knew tomorrow
you'd have forgotten it all
and we'd spend the day

watching dvds
going out for chocolate cake
searching for the cats

who never were lost
it was us lost in the now
eternal present

MARTIN

on our haiku hike
you laughed at the one about
the three-legged cat

read us your favourite
about the stone returning
home to the river

I said I'd like to
write haiku as funny and
fun as Bob Lucky

I think I bored you
banging on about Waley
Ezra Pound, Rexroth

you didn't show it
you were the patient teacher
I the keen student

NIGEL

our paths kept crossing
Wales is a little like that
remember the WASP?

we were young poets
out to sting the Arts Council
next we were playwrights

with theatres too
touring the boards to learn they
didn't want writers

then we were writing
teachers up to our elbows
in the rich gravy

you looked, sounded
like a poet—lucky for them
you were the real thing

PATSY

you were my wife's friend
she's grieving like a lover
told it's all over

no phone calls no texts
no coffee down at Wally's
no great e-mail jokes

the one about that
nun and the taxi driver
was the funniest

when I think of you
you're smiling and your smiles mean
many different things

we want more of you
the living are so greedy
but you can't blame us

PETER

you lived in the past
and tried to keep it alive
or at least intact

that was our motto
I visited Vaughan's grave on
my first trip to Wales

you and Anne brought his
poems home to this valley
the place they were born

you were soft-spoken
a courteous peaceful man
but the age you chose

to live in was full
of rage—fighting over the
future we live now

SUE

I remember you
as someone who needed help
crossing at the lights

yet had the bravest
soul I've ever encountered
I saw you put down

inveterate bores
the spectacularly rude
those who made us quail

so when it came to
disease and death you met them
head on in your style

I remember the drug
that made your hair grow—you
a cute lycanthrope

ACKNOWLEDGEMENTS

Thanks first of all to the members of my writing group, Edgeworks, for their criticism and support: Jane Blank, Deborah Kay Davies, Ruth Smith, Claire Syder

The friends, students and colleagues who have helped me with these poems or given me their support over the years are too numerous to mention, but special thanks go to:
Tiffany Atkinson, Maggie Butt, Karen Buckley, Phil Carradice, Hilary Charlesworth, Lindsay Clarke, Anne Cluysenaar, Bryn Daniel, Ann Drysdale, Roger Ellis, Carol Evans, Colin Evans, Nick Evans, Rian Evans, John Freeman, Gino Gamberini, Marion Glasscoe, Danny Gorman, David Greenslade, Sue Habeshaw, Jeremy Hooker, Claire Keegan, Hilary Llewellyn-Williams, Martin Lucas, Adrian May, Sheila Morgan, Liz Porter, Veronica Porter, Steve Prescott, Loïc Robinot, Rikky Rooksby, Ceri Rowlands, Andrew Smith, Jenny Sullivan, Jim Tucker, Pat West

Acknowledgements should go to the editors of the following:
Anglo-Welsh Review, Arcade, BBC Radio Wales, Dial-a-Poem (Welsh Arts Council), Envoi, il Cobold, Lettera, New Mexico Quarterly, New Welsh Review, Planet, Poetry Daily, Poetry New York, Poetry Nottingham, Poetry Wales, Prairie Schooner, Presence, Roundyhouse, Scintilla, Second Aeon, Sewanee Review, Southern Poetry Review
And editors of the following anthologies: Bard of the Year 1994 (Poetry Digest) Moment of Earth: Poems and Essays in Honour of Jeremy Hooker (Celtic Publications) Versatility (Tears in the Fence) The So What? Factory (Cardiff University) The Hare That Hides Within (Parthian Books) At Time's Edge: Memorial to Anne Cluysenaar.

I want to acknowledge the visual artists who have helped me produce many books, pamphlets and posters. First—simply because I have done the most work with them— Richard Cox, Jill Barker and Andy Morton. Richard has designed at least five of my books, and also produced the drawing of the Japanese hearse that appears on the cover of *Cadillac Temple,* my collection of haiku. Jill did the original wood engravings for *The Black Goddess*, my collection of sonnets, and one of her engravings I have chosen for the cover of this book. Andy did the original linocuts and cover drawing for my limericks, *How To Pronounce Welsh Place Names.*

Many thanks also go to: Peter Reddick, David Sawyer, Colin See-Paynton, Sue Shields, Ieuan Morgan Thomas, Bella Widdowson

Last, but hardly least, comes Kikusha-Ni (1753-1826) who was Japanese, a Buddhist nun who became famous for her haiku and tea ceremony. I trust she won't mind my haiku imitation.